THE ELECTRIC GOSPEL

POEMS
FOR
PUBLIC
WORSHIP

PETER DAINTY

Kevin
Mayhew

First published in 2000 by
KEVIN MAYHEW LTD
Buxhall
Stowmarket
Suffolk IP14 3BW

0 1 2 3 4 5 6 7 8 9

ISBN 1 84003 572 2
Catalogue No 1500363

Cover design by Jonathan Stroulger
Typesetting by Elisabeth Bates

To my wife, Margaret,
my lifelong friend and encourager

CONTENTS

INTRODUCTION

Electricity is an amazing power which enables us to live our lives in the complex modern world. It provides us with light, heat and energy, and makes possible industry, transport, commerce and communication on a vast scale; and any power cut immediately reminds us how much we depend upon it. But electricity can also be dangerous and shocking, and we need to approach it with due respect.

Similarly, the Gospel of Jesus Christ – his life and teaching, his passion and death, his resurrection and living Spirit – provides us with the spiritual energy to live our Christian lives today, to relate to each other in love and to seek the Kingdom of God on earth. It gives us the moral dynamic to try and live in the modern world as God wants us to live and to shape our society according to his eternal law of love. Nobody can measure the impact of Jesus Christ on human civilisation over the last two thousand years, but we know that we still need the light of his truth, the heat of his passion for righteousness and the power of his Spirit as much today as ever we did in the past.

And the same Gospel, which illuminates and enables us, also shocks – when it challenges our values, our lifestyles and our unjust systems through the lives, words and actions of prophets and saints who are inspired by a vision of better things. Then the sparks really begin to fly.

That is why this book is called *The Electric Gospel* – because most of the poems in it are inspired by the Gospel and attempt to relate it to the world we live in. They were written for use in public worship, in order to let the story of Jesus, which we hear read week after week in church, break through the barrier of familiarity and flood our own lives with its searching light. Some poems are gentle and some are harsh; some are mildly humorous, and some are not; but all are intended to be taken seriously and to stimulate thought and emotion, and maybe even action.

They are reflections on some of the themes of the Christian seasons, so most of them are arranged under the main headings of the Church's year; but in addition there is a final section containing poems and prayers for more general use. Most of the poems are companions to readings from the Bible, and so relevant Bible references are given which are essential to a proper understanding. There is also an index, which links the poems and Bible references to particular days in the Revised Common Lectionary and the Common Worship Lectionary.

The value of any poem which is meant for public as opposed to private reading, depends heavily, of course, on the way it is read – with understanding and feeling, well projected, clearly enunciated, with the right stresses in the right places, etc. This requires preparation, and will rarely be achieved if the poem is handed over five minutes before the service begins with a perfunctory, 'Would you mind reading this after the second hymn?' Preparation is even more important if several readers are involved (as is sometimes suggested; though every poem could be read by a solo reader, if preferred). Group readings can be very effective, as long as a high quality of reading is maintained by all those involved; and rehearsal in such cases is absolutely essential. Sometimes the congregation can take part in the poems by means of a chorus or response, and one poem (Turning Point) needs to be visually displayed in order to point out the significance of its shape.

Above all, the poems are meant to be enjoyable and stimulating and, like electric switches, to give access to a power which is far greater than the poems themselves.

ADVENT

GIVE US TIME

2 Corinthians 6:2

(This is a dialogue between the human race and God and could be read by two people.)

Human race:
Lord, give us the time and we'll do something great;
   we'll banish all evil and violence and hate;
   we'll march on to freedom, bring justice and peace;
   we'll feed all the hungry and warfare shall cease.
Give us time, give us time.

God:
I've given you time and what have you done?
You've marched into battle with bomb and with gun;
   you've built up your empires and revelled in war;
   you've trampled on freedom, forgotten the poor –
all the time, all the time.

Human race:
Just give us the time and we'll do and we'll dare;
   we'll transform this earth to a paradise fair;
   we'll tame all the deserts and farm all the seas,
   abolish all suffering and outlaw disease;
given time, given time.

God:
But I give you the time, and what do you do?
You scar what is beautiful, twist what is true;
   you build concrete deserts and chop down the trees;
   you poison the earth and the air and the seas.
Waste of time, waste of time.

Human race:
Only give us the time and we'll do all we can
   to conquer the world for the glory of man.
Technology's servants will spend every breath
   in reaching the stars and in mastering death,
with more time, with more time.

God:
I'll give you the time, but you'll need something more,
   if you're going to end poverty, famine and war;
   you'll need hands that are willing and hearts that are good,
   and eyes that are fixed on the Kingdom of God.
Now's the time, now's the time.

WILD JOHN

Matthew 3:1–12; Mark 1:1–8; Luke 1:11–17, 76–80; 3:1–18

Isn't it time for someone
   to shout in the desert
   like wild John;
   to come out from hiding
   in those stone cold cathedrals
   and mahogany chapels,
   to climb down
   from those polished pulpits,
   and leave those pre-conditioned
   packaged congregations?

Isn't it time for someone
   to go out and shout in the desert
   like wild John;
   someone not dressed up
   in man-made fibres,
   or driving a limousine,
   living on super-bread,
   or sleeping on Slumberland,
   or receiving ecclesiastical commission;
   but someone like wild John,
   with a wilderness diet,
   and dressed for the desert;
   apart from it all,
   where he can see it straight?

Isn't it time for someone
    to shout loud in the desert
    like wild John;
    washing the dust off our civilisation,
    before the fire comes
    and burns up the chaff;
    cleansing the dirt
    from a sordid generation
    in a river of hope,
    and bathing the wounds
    of the violent centuries,
    ready for healing?

Isn't it time for someone
    to shout in the desert
    like wild John:
'Level off the unjust hills;
    fill in the oppressed valleys;
    straighten the crooked ways
    and make a smooth road
    for the Lord to enter his Kingdom'?

KINGDOM COME

Matthew 25:1-13

Are you ready for the hour of the Kingdom,
    when the heirs of God are given their freedom,
    and the Lord acclaims those sisters and brothers,
    who have spent themselves in service of others?
For the Lord will wipe away all tears from their eyes,
    and banish all sorrow and pain and sighs,
    and even death will perish in the victory of life
    when the Kingdom of God is come.

And at midnight, when the voice of the bridegroom
    wakes us from our sleep to share in the banquet,
    will your lamp of faith be empty and smoking
    and the Lord of life say, 'I never knew you'?
For the new world's door will be open wide
    to receive those who stand by their neighbours' side
    with their lamp burning brightly till the night gives way
    to the dawn of the Day of God.

THE THREE QUESTIONS

Matthew 25:14-30; Luke 19:11-27

(This could possibly be for three readers.)

And the first question is this –
When the king returns
   and asks for an account of our stewardship,
   will there be anyone left
   with even a single talent in their hand,
   who can step forward and say:
   'I still have what you first gave me;
   not increased, to be sure,
   but certainly not diminished;
   take it back again'?
Or will the problem be
   to find any talents at all,
   buried beneath the ashes
   of a wasted world?

And the second question is this –
Will the king cast his worthless servants
   into the outer darkness,
   where there is weeping and wailing
   and gnashing of teeth?
Or will he consider it juster punishment
   to leave us in the darkness
   we have made for ourselves;
   and go in search of another world
   to try again?

And the third question is this –
   what are we going to do
   to avoid the other two questions?

ADVENT

Acts 1:9-11

Shall we gaze into the sky,
    waiting for the coming of the Christ
    who never left us?
Do we look to the heavens
    for the one who lives in our hearts?
Has he left the stage
    of the world's drama
    in order to return in triumph
    and save us all
    just in time?

Or will the flash of his appearing
    strike upon our vision
    not from the clouds above,
    but from the depths of faith and love
    in those who already see him?

CHRISTMAS

CENSUS

Luke 2:1–6

It was census day in the morning
    when Jesus Christ was born;
    and the government was
    regimenting its citizens –
    it's easier to keep people in order
    if you number them.
So Jesus came in time to be numbered
    with the man in the street –
    the Son of Almighty God,
    another card in the state filing system.
He was registered as a taxpayer,
    who would render to Caesar
    what was Caesar's.
And that's how the Son of Man became
    just an extra figure
    in the population statistics;
    an additional number
    destined, sooner or later,
    to be crossed out.

Such is the way of human government.
But God has a different method:
    he numbers the hairs on your head,
    but he calls *you* by name,
    and seeks you until he finds you,
    not to tax with heavy burdens,
    but to take the yoke upon himself
    and free you from your debts.

NO ROOM

Luke 2:7; Matthew 25:38-45

Most kings warn of their coming
   with planning committees
   and security checks, red carpets
   and well-rehearsed fanfares.
But this king always comes
   unexpectedly, and in the wrong places,
   unheralded, except by unbelievable angels.
So it was no wonder when he came
   that there was no room at the inn.
Incognito, he always surprises us,
   or passes our way unrecognised.
'When did we see you, Lord?' we ask;
   and he answers:
'There was a pregnant woman
   looking for a decent place to have her baby
   and only finding a stable;
   there was an innocent man
   staring down from a cross,
   searching for humanity
   and finding no room in your hearts.'

HE HUMBLED HIMSELF

Luke 2:7; Philippians 2:6-7

The new-born king arrived
    at twelve o'clock midnight precisely
    (Middle Eastern Time),
    a rather feeble 4lbs 5oz
    (but what could you expect
    from an undernourished peasant girl?)
No district nurse was present;
    there was no delivery bed,
    no injections,
    no gas and air,
    no shiny, sterile instruments,
    no hints on correct breathing,
    no attendant doctors;
    only soiled straw, and cobwebs,
    and staring animals
    and a farmyard smell;
    and awkward Joseph's shaking hand,
    holding a shivering lamp
    for the innkeeper's wife,
    who was busy
    with her rough, well-meaning fingers.

So the new red king entered his kingdom
　　to the pricking of hay, and the tight warmth
　　of the long swathing bandage.
There was no dignity about it,
　　except the dignity that attends
　　every human birth;
　　no mystery, except the normal mystery
　　of a new life; no wonder
　　except the wonder of excited shepherds
　　with half-mad stories of angelic visions.

For God stooped low, and will stoop lower,
　　even to the oozy bottom of the human ocean,
　　to raise the sunken treasure
　　of lost souls.

THE SHEPHERDS

Luke 2:8-20

The shepherds watched their flocks by night,
   and saw angels –
   while townsmen, sleeping
   in a noisier, narrower world,
   blinkered against the light,
   deaf to eternal voices,
   waking only to complete the daily schedule,
   saw and heard
   nothing.

And the shepherds,
   seeing angels,
   did not then disperse the vision
   with cool reason,
   raising mental barricades
   to blot out the light,
   but received the message
   with unquestioning joy,
   open-mouthed,
   yet speechless.

And these same poor shepherds,
    unembarrassed by the stable
    and the Saviour's poverty,
    gladly adored him,
    overawed by the very lowliness
    which would have repelled
    those richer in possessions,
    but with ragged souls.

So the shepherds,
    being ready to receive from God with honest faith,
    were as wise in their way
    as the bringers of gold, frankincense and myrrh.

PLEASE DO NOT ADJUST

Luke 2:8-14; John 1:10-11

While people watched their sets one night,
  all seated round the screen,
  the angel of the Lord appeared
  where evening news had been.
'Fear not,' said he (for flashing lights
  had altered the transmission;
  this strange, celestial visitor
  had interfered with vision).
'I bring good news of peace on earth
  for all mankind,' he said;
  but crackling sparks zig-zagged the screen
  and every set went dead.
So angry viewers growled and cursed
  and electricians fumed,
  until as soon as possible
  normal service was resumed.

BLESSED ARE THE MEEK

Matthew 5:5

Though proud men ruled the world,
　enthroned in pomp and power,
　the plan of God unfurled
　in a fragile village flower,
　an unsophisticated girl,
　who dared say 'Yes' to God's strange will.

Those rich men did not know,
　wrapped in cocoons of gold,
　that, where the raw winds blow,
　God's message was being told
　to poor men watching through the night,
　bedazzled by mysterious light.

And those with earthbound eyes
　could never understand
　that God accounted wise
　men from a distant land,
　who searched the heavens for signs of grace
　and chased a star to see God's face.

The great ones have their day
　and strut this worldly stage,
　while God prepares a play
　fit for a different age,
　when wooden cross and stable birth
　empower the meek to rule the earth.

GOD WITH US

Matthew 1:23

In answer to our searching
    and our fear of being alone,
    God entered human history
    in the person of his Son.
The Word that brought the world to be
    was heard in Galilee.
The voice that said, 'Let there be light'
    cried out on Calvary.
The feet that danced when time began
    now walked in dust and blood.
The hand that formed the galaxies
    was nailed to a cross of wood.

For God said, 'I am with you.
    I came in flesh and bone
    to show you that I love you
    and you'll never be alone.'

LOOK ON THIS CHILD

John 1:14

(This could be for three readers.)

Look on this child with awe, here is a mystery;
   not a concoction only of molecules and genes,
   (though that in itself is miracle),
   but the essence of the past,
   distilled in one small life;
   the latest fruit of nature's ancient tree.

Look on this child with love; love is its birthright;
   it was conceived in love, however strange,
   and will be nurtured best in love,
   just as the flower blooms best
   that is most cared for;
   hate and neglect will wither; love gives life.

Look on this child with hope; it could just be
   that this one gives the lie to all our faults,
   and, unlike us, learns from past failures.
If ever dreams come true,
   why should they not come true
   with this appearing of a new-born hope?

WE CELEBRATE

Philippians 2:5-11

(For up to seven readers.)

We celebrate the birth of Jesus Christ,
   son of a carpenter, now honoured as a king.
Born in the night and murdered in dark day,
   his light shines on across the years
   and searches everything.

We celebrate the truth taught by a man
   whose words have outlived empires and outstretched the wise.
His moral vision challenges the world;
   his simple Gospel has the power
   to heal and civilise.

We celebrate the love which drove his life,
   embracing sinners and relieving desperate needs.
His love burns still in all those servant saints,
   whose deep concerns and passionate prayers
   are matched by costly deeds.

We celebrate the faith and peace and hope
   which Christ has brought to countless followers of his Way.
A faith which lights the road, an inner peace
   which steels the soul, and hope which looks
   with joy towards the day.

He did not come to show the light of God
  in power and wealth, but in weak flesh and blood of death.
We see God's light in Christ's humanity:
  he called himself the Son of Man
  and came from Nazareth.

Our global warming world of fragile dreams
  hopes truly for the best, yet fears the worst might be.
May we not turn our faces from the light,
  but seek God's justice, peace and good
  in earth and sky and sea.

Artists have caught the radiant light of Christ
  in paint and music, words and wood and chiselled stone.
But turning our dull clay to Spirit's gold
  is work befitting Christ the Master
  Craftsman's skill alone.

EPIPHANY

WISE MEN'S GIFTS

Matthew 2:1–12

Whatever happened to the Magi's gold, Lord Jesus?
Did it fall into the hands of Herod's men,
   when you fled from Bethlehem?
Or maybe it dropped off the back of a camel
   on the road into Egypt
   and was picked up by the greedy fingers
   of a passing merchant?
Otherwise, how does that gold,
   symbol of the whole wealth of the whole world,
   given to you by wise men for safe keeping,
   now come to be in the hands of the minions of Mammon,
   the manipulators of money markets,
   the profiteers and speculators,
   the fraudulent, the affluent and the corpulent?
Surely this is not what it means when it says
   that you became poor, that we might become rich.
Call on new wise men, O Christ,
   to give you back your gold,
   because it's burning holes in humanity.

And what about the frankincense, Lord,
   symbol of religion?
Did your mother drop it in the Temple,
   to be claimed by the authorities
   and piped down a succession of priests and prophets,
   crowd-stirrers and heart-throbs,
   its mesmerising smoke wafting by the nostrils
   of centuries of idols,
   to the accompaniment of holy turnstile music?
Take back the frankincense, O Christ,
   before we are choked by the stink
   of the worship of false gods.

But the myrrh, the symbol of death,
   and most unlikely of birthday presents,
   you did not lose.
You kept it, without ever needing it;
   for, having died,
   your body could not be found to be embalmed,
   and you could not simply be preserved
   as a fragrant memory.
Instead, your living Spirit strides the world,
   looking for those who are wise enough
   to give you back the incense and the gold.

THE INNOCENTS

Matthew 2:13-23; John 1:10

(For up to five readers.)

What do we do with the babe in the cradle;
　the babe in the cradle, the hope of the world?
House it in shanty town, hovel and stable;
　a refugee camp for the hope of the world.

How do we care for the infant so helpless;
　the infant so helpless, the young one so frail?
Give it no doctors, no fit sanitation;
　and raise it in squalor, the young one so frail.

How do we nourish the seed of the future;
　the seed of the future, the heir of mankind?
Feed it with charity soya bean mixture;
　a cupful of rice for the heir of mankind.

How do we nurture the child full of promise;
　the child full of promise, the light of the world?
School it in prejudice, half truths and falsehood;
　and quench with dark hatred the light of the world.

Where are the wise men with gifts for the baby;
　with gifts for a baby, but fit for a king?
Bring him the best of the world's wealth, and maybe
　our great expectations will blossom in him.
Treat him with reverence, the tender young sapling;
　then great expectations will blossom in him.

THE BOY IN THE TEMPLE

Luke 2:41-52

Beware, old men,
   of the boy who asks questions
   in the Temple.
Beware of his probing mind,
   like the prodding finger of God
   unplayfully poking holes
   in your ancient dignity.
Hide those antique laws
   before he sees the spirit
   beneath the letter.
Protect those sacred truths with iron fear,
   or he will fan them into life
   with the breath of his living faith;
   and the fire of their knowledge
   will destroy both you
   and your solemn system.
Beware of this boy who asks questions,
   the inquisitive Son
   of a disturbing Father.

[Continued

Others there are
   whom you need not fear –
   they ask no questions,
   but tread traditional ways
   like sleep-walkers, blindly following
   the easy path of custom,
   each predictable today
   a reprint of a ritual yesterday.

But this boy,
   who so amazes with his insight,
   is stirring the dust of ages
   with the eternal broom of truth,
   for he is God's boy,
   already about his Father's business.

LENT

THE TEMPTATIONS

Matthew 4:1-11; Mark 1:12-13; Luke 4:1-13

(This could be shared between several readers.)

When Jesus was hungry, the Devil said,
   'Turn these dry stones into bread.
There's no need to starve when with your power
   you could grind these pebbles into flour.
Hear those hungry people cry;
   are you so heartless as to let them die?
Think of the world in all its need;
   what a saviour you'd be if you gave them bread.'

But Jesus looked in silence
   to the far horizon
   and saw . . .
   you and me, in our complacency.
With our bakeries full of bread,
   and our superstores full of bread,
   and our freezers full of bread,
   and our bellies full of bread;
   oven-fresh, ready-sliced,
   fibre-filled bread;
   and the pieces left over
   were gathered up
   for waste disposal,
   but not for the hungry.

For we had learned
   to turn stones into bread.
But we still had stony faces without joy
   and stony hearts without love;
   while the world was starving for justice.

So Jesus turned back to the Devil and said,
   'I will not turn these stones into bread.
For everyone but you must own
   that man shall not live by bread alone.
And the only thing that really feeds
   is the Word that from God's mouth proceeds.'

Then the Devil tried a different tack
   in order our Lord's will to crack.
He took him to a Temple tower
   and showed him how to get great power:
   by throwing himself from this high steeple
   he would dazzle and amaze the people,
   for angels just in time would fly
   to hold him up lest he should die.

But Jesus looked in silence
   to the far horizon
   and saw . . .
   you and me, in our credulity;
   how we were blinded
   by the glitter of our gods,
   so that open-mouthed
   we could see and believe
   anything but the Truth
   (which is invisible
   and requires inner eyes).

[Continued

And he saw that
   we had great confidence in tricks,
   and we unwisely followed the stars,
   and we were deafened
   by the purring of public relations
   and swayed
   to the music of mass communications.
And we were the unthinking people,
   spellbound
   by the charisma of false images.

So he turned to the Devil
   and snapped his reply,
   'It shall not be my way to lie,
   and trick and smile and hypnotise
   and wear a conjuror's disguise,
   and use the gift of heavenly power
   to gain men's praise for one brief hour.
What Scripture says is plain and best:
   "You shall not put God to the test."'

But the Devil was not beaten yet;
   he took Jesus from that parapet
   to the top of a mountain where clouds unfurled,
   revealing the kingdoms of the world.
'All that,' said the Devil, 'I'll give to you,
   if you bow to me with worship true.'

But Jesus looked in silence
   to the far horizon
   and saw . . .
   you and me, in our degeneracy,
   bowing beneath the Devil's heavy load,
   having received power to become
   lords of the earth.

He heard the excuses of the exploiters,
   and the explanations of the polluters;
   he saw self-promoting empires,
   and self-infatuated tyrants,
   and self-justifying politicians,
   and self-righteous people
   shrugging technological shoulders
   at the poisoned earth,
   while consumers consumed
   and populations exploded
   the myth of the world's abundance,
   and everybody minded their own business
   greedily.

Then Jesus in anger,
   in red-blooded anger,
   cut the Devil down to size.
He glared at him with blazing eyes
   and asked him who gave him the right
   to dole out this world's wealth and might
   and call on all the human race
   to bow down low before his face.
For only one God reigns above;
   him only should we serve and love.
'So, begone Satan!' Jesus cried,
   'with your foul conspiracies I'll not side.'

Then angels came to help our Lord
   with heavenly power to preach the Word,
   and live a life of burning love
   which all this aching world would move.

WATER INTO WINE

John 2:1-11

When the wine runs dry
   at the festival of life,
   when words fail, and music dies;
   when our joys wear thin,
   or old friendships end in strife,
   and our laughter turns to sighs –

   then come, Lord Jesus,
   turn our water into wine,
   as you turn the rain from heaven
   to the sweetness of the vine;
   turn the tears of our night
   into songs of the day,
   and revive us with your Spirit
   as we walk the pilgrim way;
   and baptise us with a fresh desire
   to love you and obey –
Jesus, turn our water into wine.

When you took your towel and bowl
   and you washed those weary feet,
   you turned that water into wine.
And when we, at your command,
   give a cup to cool the heat,
   you turn that water into wine.
So come, Lord Jesus,
   bring your heaven down to earth,
   and fulfil the ancient prophecy
   that at the world's new birth
   every tear will be dried up
   and there will be no more sea;
   for we understand the reason
   why such wonders have to be –
   it's because you'll have completed
   what began in Galilee:
   you'll have turned all the water into wine.

THE FISHERMEN'S SONG

Mark 1:16-20; Luke 5:1-11; Mark 6:47-51; Mark 4:35-41

(The congregation could join in the chorus of this one.)

We were sitting by the seashore
   mending our nets,
   just to make an honest living
   and to pay all our debts,
   when a voice from the blue
   woke us from our reverie:
'Leave your nets where they are, boys,
   and come and follow me.'

'And I will make you to become
   real fishermen for me.'

And when people heard him preaching
   the word of the Lord,
   they were crowding by the lake side
   where our vessels were moored.
Jesus gave us a shout
   as he took off his coat:
'It would help me a lot, boys,
   if I could use your boat.'

'And I will make you to become
   real fishermen for me.'

We had spent the long night fishing
    far out on the deep,
    and we hadn't caught a thing
    and were ready for sleep.
But the Lord turned us back,
    saying: 'Boys, just try again.'
And the catch was so great, we
    could hardly drag it in.

'And I will make you to become
    real fishermen for me.'

We were making heavy weather
    caught out in a storm,
    clinging fast to the rigging,
    praying hard for the dawn;
    when the Master appeared,
    walking calmly on the waves,
    calling: 'Don't you believe, boys,
    that God's the one who saves?'

'And I will make you to become
    real fishermen for me.'

We were sailing with the Master
    asleep in the stern,
    when the sky grew black and stormy
    and the wind took a turn.
But the Master arose,
    when he heard of our alarm,
    and the power of his word made
    the wind and waters calm.

'And I will make you to become
    real fishermen for me.'

WELCOME

Matthew 13:53-58; Mark 6:1-5; Luke 4:16-30

(For up to five readers.)

Jesus Christ is welcome in his own home town,
  where we bask in the sunshine of his fame.
He is Joseph's son, the joiner,
  and of all of Nazareth's lads
  he's the only one who ever made a name.
We will rest on his laurels;
  we will gloat on his success,
  as the tourists flock the market,
  as the crowds begin to press;
  and when Jesus has passed on
  we'll still sell Jesus souvenirs;
  he's the best thing that has happened
  in a thousand million years.

Jesus Christ is welcome in his own home town,
  when he goes to worship on the Sabbath day.
Our habitual religion
  gets a comfortable boost
  with the presence of our hero while we pray.
He supports our age-old customs,
  he reveres our hallowed ways,
  as he reads the ancient prophet,
  as he speaks of better days.
He will help defend morality,
  make decent people glad.
He will keep this town respectable;
  our own dear village lad.

But Jesus isn't welcome in his own home town,
    when he starts to pass harsh judgement on his kin.
It is one thing to inspire us
    with his gracious words of hope,
    quite another to accuse us all of sin.
How dare he come among us
    making wild, outrageous claims?
He was brought up in the alleys
    where we played our childhood games.
Does this upstart think he's better
    than the folk he's left at home?
Then we'll cast him out for evermore!
We'll give him 'kingdom come'!

So Jesus passed among them
    and went on his lonely way,
    shaking all the dust of bitterness from his feet.
But the prejudice and fear which sought
    his blood were not content
    till they'd driven him from every lane and street.
And outside a city wall
    he was excluded from that place,
    and was forced to die with criminals
    in shame and in disgrace.
But he's opened up a Kingdom
    filled with God's unbounded grace,
    in which welcome for the outcast
    is complete.

[Continued

Therefore Jesus Christ will welcome
   to his own home town
   every sad and weary stranger,
   every child laid in a manger,
   every friendless, homeless creature,
   every wandering, love-filled preacher,
   all who suffer dreadful loss,
   all who end up on a cross;
   and their joy will banish gloom
   when they rise up from the tomb
   in the Kingdom of the Lord,
   which is their home.

THE WANDERER

Matthew 8:19-20; Luke 9:57-58

A fox has a hole
   and a bird has a nest
   but Jesus has nowhere
   to lie down and rest.
He travels the earth
   like a clown or a tramp,
   and he knows what it's like
   in a refugee camp.

Jesus, wanderer,
   travelling alone;
   knocking on doors
   in search of a home.

He's one with the outcast
   who's branded at birth.
He's one with the stranger
   and pilgrim on earth.
He's one with the poor man
   of no fixed address.
He sits with the lonely
   and shares their distress.

Jesus, wanderer,
   travelling alone;
   knocking on doors
   in search of a home.

THE BEATITUDES

Matthew 5:1-12

(Suitable for up to nine readers.)

In the kingdom of Mammon they firmly believe
    that happiness is a cigar,
    an expensive meal, a successful deal,
    or a luxury motor car.
But the Kingdom of heaven belongs to the poor
    who want no more.

In the kingdom of Mammon they laugh and they sing
    to the promptings of pleasure machines;
    they are grimly resolved to enjoy every hour
    and perpetuate youth by all means.
But God gives true comfort to all those who mourn
    and are reborn.

In the kingdom of Mammon they know how to rule
    with arrogant metallic powers;
    they scan the horizon with violent eyes
    from distant electronic towers.
But God has apportioned this earth to the meek,
    who gently seek.

In the kingdom of Mammon they hunger and thirst
    for possessions and pleasure and power;
    and though the first taste may be sweet to the tongue,
    their increase is putrid and sour.
But those who crave good are eternally filled,
    as God has willed.

In the kingdom of Mammon the law of the state
   is enforced with an iron intent;
    the offender is crushed with the harshest revenge
    that justice's slaves can invent.
But God reserves mercy for those who forgive,
   glad to let live.

In the kingdom of Mammon they search for the truth
   in a million mystical ways:
    from magic and trances to dangerous drugs,
    and the latest nonsensible craze.
But God shines on those who combine a pure heart
   with childlike art.

In the kingdom of Mammon they're masters of war
   with their missiles and bombers and guns;
    they are always prepared for surprising attacks
    and the blazing of nuclear suns.
But the children of God are the ones who make peace;
   may they increase.

In the kingdom of Mammon they torture and kill
   for the sake of the popular good;
    any threat to the state will be jailed without trial
    or nailed to a blunt cross of wood.
But God's Kingdom belongs to all those who endure,
   faithful and sure.

The kingdom of Mammon looks noble and grand
   in the glare of technology's day,
    but its concrete foundations are rooted in sand
    and are ready to crumble away.
The Kingdom of Heaven is founded on rock;
   proof against shock.

AGE OF MIRACLES

Matthew 14:15-21; Mark 6:35-44; Luke 9:12-17; John 6:5-13

Now that Man is the master of things
    miracles don't happen, naturally,
    but they do happen artificially.
We can walk on water at will
    by ski or hovercraft;
    and give the blind their sight
    by corneal graft.
The neurosurgeon's knife
    can cure paralysis;
    and devils fly in fear
    from psychoanalysis.
For Man is the master of things
    and miracles happen
    by appointment.

Even virgin births are conceived
    by test tube insemination;
    while death is dispersed with a kiss,
    or transplantation.
When in rockets we reach for the skies,
    it's in shuttles, not in angels,
    that earthbound safety lies.
For Man is the master of things,
    and miracles happen
    mechanically.

Why then,
    proud miracle worker,
    why then can you not find
    sufficient sliced loaves
    and fish fingers
    to feed the multitudes?

EASY IS THE WAY

Luke 13:22-30

Easy is the way that leads to life,
    through the gates of the Kingdom,
    where admission is free
    and the Father runs to greet you with a kiss.
Easy is the way that leads to life,
    but few there be that believe it.

For the other way is hard
    and seems more fitting –
    the way of discipline and self-denial,
    the hair shirt and the bed of nails;
    the way of ritual and right religion,
    fine prayers and costly gifts;
    the moral way of strenuous goodness
    and careful respectability;
    the intellectual way of tortuous reason,
    intense debate and learned books
    and the earnest search for truth.

But that way,
    that broad and steep way,
    that proud and noble highway,
    is the way that leads to destruction
    in the depths of despair,
    where all is vanity.

It is the easier way that leads to life:
   the way of acceptance;
   the narrow way
   that allows us to bring no gifts,
   but empty-handed
   to receive from God.
This is the way of the bird with the air;
   the way of the fish with the sea;
   the way of the seed with the soil and the rain.
It is the way of the child
   with the baptismal waters.
For as we came into the world naked,
   so must we enter the Kingdom of God,
   to be born again into his family.

Easy is the way that leads to life –
   if it *is* easy to leave behind
   all the clutter of self-justification,
   and enter into the Kingdom
   with nothing.

CONTACT

Matthew 8:1-3; Mark 1:40-42; Luke 5:12-13

Jesus was not afraid
  to touch people;
  not with the formal handshake of greeting,
  or the limp clasp of indifference;
  not with the vicious jab of hate,
  the lascivious stroke of lust,
  or greed's sweaty clutch;
  but with the gentle touch
  of fingers on blind eyes,
  deaf ears and speechless tongues;
  the touch that healed.
His reassuring grasp
  cleansed scaly leprous hands.
His grip was strong enough
  to put the lame on their feet
  and free the paralysed.

Let those of us
  whose fingers touch, not other fingers,
  but computer buttons;
  who hide behind a barrier
  of printed words,
  instructions and reports
  or the armchair newspaper;
  who never actually meet
  the needs of our neighbour,
  except through collection boxes
  held in the gloved hands of charity;

who are divided from others
by stone walls
or wooden pews
or windscreens
and well-trimmed hedges,
remember that Jesus Christ,
the Word made flesh,
the very hand of God,
was not afraid to touch
people.

Nor was Jesus afraid
to be touched
by people;
not just the accidental jostle
of the anonymous crowd
(though even that could help);
nor the playful prods of children
(though he would not turn them away),
but even the soldiers' rough brutality,
the stinging slaps and cold spittle
of Pilate's grinning henchmen;
the bitter kiss of a traitor,
and the burning talons
of the crucifiers.

So Christ's Body still
reaches out to those
who ache for love.
Nor should it shrink back
from the world's unfeeling blows,
but, turning cheek,
use even that as
saving contact.

HANDS

Matthew 15:1-2, 10-20; Mark 7:1-5, 14-23

(For up to six readers.)

Jesus the carpenter used his hands,
   he used his hands to make and to mend.
As he laboured to learn his father's old trade,
   with sawdust and sweat his hands were ingrained.

Simon the Pharisee washed his hands,
   he washed his hands when he sat down to eat.
But Jesus his guest ate with hands that were stained
   from healing the sick in the dusty street.

Pilate the Governor washed his hands,
   he washed his hands of innocent blood.
But such was the guilt that dirtied his soul,
   he might well have washed his hands in mud.

Jesus the crucified stretched his hands,
   he stretched his hands in sorrow and love.
And though they were twisted with iron and pain,
   they shone with a glory from heaven above.

Who shall ascend the hill of the Lord,
   and who shall stand in his holy place?
'The man with clean hands,' the Psalmist said,
   but Jesus has proved that isn't the case.

For hands that are scented and washed and clean,
   protected from toil in a fancy glove,
   are never as pure in the eyes of the Lord
   as the hands that are soiled in service and love.

LET THE CHILDREN COME

Matthew 19:13-15; Mark 10:13-16; Luke 18:15-17

When mothers brought their children
    to sit on Jesus' knee,
    his followers turned them all away;
    said, 'We've no time to stop and play;
    we're doing Kingdom work today;
    go home and let us be.'

When Jesus saw the children,
    he called them to his side;
    he said, 'The Kingdom is your home,
    and those who want to enter in,
    must all, like you, be born again
    and leave behind their pride.'

When children came to Jesus,
    they did not understand
    the language of theology,
    or sound ecclesiology –
    they came without apology
    and took him by the hand.

THE GREAT DIVIDE

Luke 16:19-31

The rich man feasted all the day long,
    while the poor man lay at his door.
The rich man's body was sleek and fat,
    while the poor man's was thin and sore.
The rich man's clothes were costly and fine
    but the poor man's were dirty and worn.
O save us, Lord, from this great divide
    into which rich and poor are born.

May we who are rich learn to share our wealth
    with the poor who lie at our gate;
    and use our abundance for everyone's good,
    before we discover too late
    that the time has come when the great divide,
    that separates rich from poor,
    has become the divide between heaven and hell –
    and we're the wrong side of the door.

Lord, help us to pull *all* the barriers down
    that threaten our social health:
    the walls of colour and sex and creed,
    of nationhood and of wealth.
Prevent us from turning the human race
    to a warring and cancerous cell,
    which reduces the planet to nuclear dust
    in the fires of a man-made hell.

We've failed to respond to your message of doom
   in all that the prophets have said;
   but now, in your mercy, you've sent us new hope,
   through the preacher who rose from the dead.
May we hear his voice; may we follow his way;
   may we learn what leads to peace;
   may his beautiful Kingdom of justice and love
   for ever and ever increase.

HOLY WEEK

THREE CHEERS FOR JESUS

Matthew 21:8-15; John 19:1-5; Matthew 27:35-44

(For up to five readers.)

Three cheers for Jesus!
He comes to be our king.
He'll overthrow the tyrants,
   and wealth and freedom bring.
He'll outlaw every evil –
   all pain and fear and greed.
He'll take over the government
   and meet our every need.

Two cheers for Jesus.
He claims to be our king,
   but he's striding through the Temple
   and upsetting everything.
He's scattering our profits
   and the businesses we've made;
   is he really fit to rule us
   if he spoils our holy trade?

One cheer for Jesus.
He came to be our king,
    but now he stands on trial,
    red with the whip's sharp sting.
With crown of thorns they mock him,
    scorned by official power.
He's helpless with authority;
    this cannot be his hour.

No cheers for Jesus.
He's surely not our king.
They've nailed him to a wooden cross
    while people laugh and sing.
The one we thought would save us
    they curse and wound and kill.
Our hopes and expectations
    die with him on that hill.

Now heaven cheers for Jesus.
The world has had its say;
    and God has raised him from the dead –
    there dawns another day.
Disciples stand bewildered
    beside an empty grave,
    but soon they will be cheering too
    for the Christ who came to save.

AGONY IN THE GARDEN

Luke 22:39-46, 23:42-43

As you kneel there in the garden
  in the coldness of the night,
  and you contemplate the terror
  of the quenching of the light,
  do you think back to that garden –
  and I speak now like a child –
  to that perfect heaven, which was your home,
  that Paradise undefiled,
  and remember how you trembled
  with your love for this poor earth,
  as you emptied all your self
  into that lowly stable birth:
  the first step of a journey
  through this world of sin and power,
  on the path of loving service
  which has brought you to this hour?
Do you remember how you left behind
  that glorious world of light,
  as you kneel there in the garden,
  in the coldness of the night?

As you fall in prayer upon the grass
    of dark Gethsemane,
    are you thinking of that story
    of the serpent and the tree?
Just a story known from childhood,
    now rewritten in your life –
    through the agony of temptation
    and the sweat of inner strife.
As you ask if God is willing
    to remove the cup of pain,
    does the memory of Eden
    steel your heart to think again,
    and to bow before your calling
    as the Father's loving Son,
    and to say in calm acceptance:
'Not my will, but yours, be done?'

Lord, we thank you for your courage
    and we thank you for your love;
    we have failed in our own Eden,
    we're not fit for heaven above;
    but we dare to claim the mercy
    promised to the dying thief
    as he cried out, 'Lord, remember me!'
    in penitence and grief;
    and you answered in your pity,
'Come with me to Paradise';
    then submitted to the Father,
    as you paid the sinner's price.

DENIAL

Matthew 26:31-35, 69-75; Mark 14:27-31, 66-72
Luke 22:31-34, 54-62; John 18:15-18, 25-27

Lord, forgive us,
  that, like Peter,
  we can swear we do not know you
  even louder than we swore
  when we said we'd never leave you.

Lord, forgive us:
Lord, forgive us.

Lord, forgive us
  when our courage
  is a thing of bluff and bluster,
  which, when someone calls our bluff,
  soon dissolves in tears and fluster.

Lord, forgive us:
Lord, forgive us.

Lord, forgive us
  when we praise you
  with our lips, but not our action;
  may the cock crow wake us up
  from our blind self-satisfaction.

Lord, forgive us:
Lord, forgive us.

Lord, redeem us
   when we fail you
   not just three times, but more often;
   may our conscience not grow hard,
   lest it grow too hard to soften.

Lord, redeem us:
Lord, redeem us.

When hosannas
   turn to catcalls
   and we're tempted to deny you,
   give us faith that will not fade
   and the courage to stand by you.

Keep us faithful:
Keep us faithful.

GF
2019

THE TRIAL

John 18:12-14, 19-24, 28-40; 19:1-16

When Jesus Christ was tried in Palestine,
  two charges were considered by the courts:
  first, that he posed a threat to Church and God;
  second, he was a danger to the State.
But neither accusation could they prove,
  and Christ's conviction was unjustified.

What did those giants have to fear from him –
  the Son of David, armed with nought but love?
Do priests and temples, kings and empires shake
  before the man whose crown is twisted thorns?

Yet maybe Caiaphas and Pilate knew
  that Jesus had a greater strength than theirs:
  a message set to win the common heart
  and shake the unjust powers from their thrones;
  a Spirit which would fire the human soul
  and burn away the dross of inborn sin;
  a love to bear all suffering and wrong
  and build a kingdom out of truth and good.

The influence of Jesus on this world
  cannot be measured, nor is yet complete;
  for whereas those who tried him are long gone,
  his living presence stirs our spirits still.
And though our Lord seemed helpless, when he stood
  in mocking robe of purple stained with red,
  it is not he who stands on trial now,
  but Church, and State, and every mortal soul.

And though he is a king, he does not rule
   by force of arms, or wealth's persuasive power;
   but by the seeming weakness of his love,
   he gains an entrance to the human heart.
As he himself declared, it is the meek
   to whom God, in his pleasure, gives the earth.

FRIDAY

Mark 15:25-39

It was bad Friday on Golgotha hill
    when they set up a cross in order to kill.
They nailed through the hands
    and they nailed through the feet
    of the man of love to whom life was sweet;
    and his blood washed away
    in the tears of the rain,
    and the very earth shook
    with the shame of his pain.
It was bad Friday on Golgotha hill
    when they set up a cross
    in order to kill.

It was bad Friday on Golgotha hill,
    when they murdered a man for doing God's will.
His tongue was dry
    and his throat was hoarse,
    but the clamour of men
    was strident and coarse;
    and black was the earth
    and black was the sky
    when the Truth was stretched
    on a cross to die.
It was bad Friday on Golgotha hill
    when they murdered a man
    for doing God's will.

It was bad Friday on Golgotha hill,
   when the voices of love and of truth were still.
And a duty was done
   for the good of the state
   outside the respectable city gate;
   and the world was ruled
   for those six evil hours
   by the pride and the greed
   of corrupt human powers.
It was bad Friday on Golgotha hill
   when the voices of love and of truth
   were still.

But now we can see with a clearer eye
   the power of a man who was ready to die.
For the light that was hid
   and the life that was lost
   have won for the world,
   at a measureless cost,
   the ultimate triumph
   of truth and of good
   against all the worst tortures
   of iron and wood.
So that bad Friday on Golgotha hill
   became Good Friday then,
   and is Good Friday still.

THE CROSS

1 Peter 2:24 (RSV, NIV)

It's bad enough to hang a man
　　by the neck until he's dead;
　　worse to use a green leaf tree
　　as your instrument of dread;
　　worse still when the tree is hacked,
　　sawn and fashioned as a cross –
　　agony is then its fruit,
　　flesh its bark and blood its moss.
Rootless, stark, it stabs the earth;
　　leafless, heeds no wind or breath;
　　wooden instrument of pain,
　　man's creation: Tree of Death.

But a brighter truth now dawns.
God reverses our black arts;
　　breathes life into wood and nails
　　as the re-creation starts.
Roots strike deep in earth's rich heart,
　　making firm against the wind.
Buds unfold in faith's warm sun:
　　healing leaves for humankind.
Sheltering boughs fill all the sky,
　　branches all the world embrace.
Evergreen, God's Tree of Life
　　bears sweet fruit of love and grace.

From a tree they made a cross,
　　in their blind iniquity.
God alone redeems that loss –
　　turns the cross into a tree.

THE LAST THROW OF THE DICE

Mark 12:1-8; John 19:28-30

The last move in the game
   was very like the first
   in some things;
   his death was like his birth –
   poor, weak, naked, in the dark,
   stared at by animals,
   innocent victim of ignorance,
   his body linen-wrapped
   and laid to rest;
   and still there was no room.

But it was different too;
   a *public* humiliation –
   the crowds had gathered
   for the finish;
   not excited shepherds
   with light in their eyes,
   but scowling spectators,
   bored soldiers
   and stone-faced priests;
   and no angel music,
   but the hate-filled howlings
   of a callous mob;
   no prickling straw,
   but piercing thorns and nails;
   no precious gifts,

but a sponge full of bitter wine;
and no wise worshippers,
but weeping women and empty disciples
and Mary with a breaking heart.

So the last stake was raised,
   and the dice that God threw at Bethlehem
   came to rest on Calvary –
   the gamble of his love
   to win a world.

AUTUMN

Mark 15:46

When the last seed breaks away
   from the November tree,
   swaying a lonely waltz
   in the misty sunset,
   and coming to rest
   among the mouldering remnants
   of the Fall,
   I think of Jesus,
   gently borne down
   from his bare tree,
   the fragile reject
   of a wintry world.
And I know that his burial
   is the planting of a Kingdom,
   and that all is now ready
   for the coming spring.

THE BURIAL

John 19:38-42

Jesus is not buried by his enemies,
    but by his friends –
    not by Caiaphas and Pilate,
    but by Joseph and Nicodemus;
    not by atheists and unbelievers,
    but by those who love him.
It is his followers who seek
    to lay him reverently to rest.

They bury him deep
    under mountains of tradition,
    safely entomb him
    in the narrow coffin of religion.
They wrap him up tight
    in the protective shroud of dogma,
    preferring funereal ritual
    to resurrection joy,
    and a dim religious light
    to the eye-stinging brightness
    of God's good morning.

[Continued

The tears are genuine,
　　and the precious ointment of fine words,
　　preserving the fragrant memory
　　of a mummified saviour.
But the heavy stone
　　they roll across the tomb
　　is the stone of fear –
　　fear of the living God.
God-in-a-box
　　is not as disturbing
　　as God in the world.

Yet they may as well try
　　to bury the wind,
　　for he is free and alive,
　　and his devoted guardians
　　cannot hold him down,
　　however grave their intentions.

EASTER

TURNING POINT

Acts 2:23-24

(If possible, this should be displayed visually.)

On the first Good Friday
disciples silent stood;
weary women weeping;
thorns drew blood;
crowd spat loud;
earth shook;
black sky;
red wood;
soldiers
nailed
God.

Then,
three days
pregnant dark,
earth shakes again,
sets free its treasure,
as Christ escapes the tomb
at God the Father's pleasure.
Bright sky, spring flowers bloom;
now soldiers faint, disciples run about,
and women shout good news of joy beyond measure.

HALLELUJAH!

Matthew 28:1-3; John 20:19-20; Revelation 19:6

When the Lord of life was dead,
  day had turned to blackest night.
It seemed as though the whole world bled,
  drained of hope and joy and light.

Yet it wasn't long
  before they heard this song:

Hallelujah! Christ is risen!
Hallelujah! Christ is Lord!
Night is ended. Day is breaking.
Hallelujah! Christ is Lord!

When disciples met in fear,
  huddled in an upper room,
Jesus came and showed his wounds;
  peace and joy dispersed their gloom.

And it wasn't long
  before they sang this song:

Hallelujah! Christ is risen!
Hallelujah! Christ is Lord!
Night is ended. Day is breaking.
Hallelujah! Christ is Lord.

[Continued

When we enter darkest night,
   threatening shadows all around,
   we'll catch a glimpse of radiant light,
   feel the beat of distant sound.

Then it won't be long
   before we'll hear this song:

Hallelujah! Christ is risen!
Hallelujah! Christ is Lord!
Night is ended. Day is breaking.
Hallelujah! Christ is Lord!

CHICKS

John 19:41-20:1

When chickens hatch out of their eggs
    and stand on their spindly legs,
    chirping a cheery song
    in the new world to which they belong,
    they remind me of Easter Day,
    when the Lord Jesus broke away
    out of the dreary tomb,
    in a garden where flowers bloom;
    and the birds sang a loud song of praise
    to the God who alone can raise
    a man from the grip of death,
    and give to a chick new breath.

THE ROAD TO EMMAUS

Luke 24:13-35

(For two readers, representing the two disciples.)

Cleopas: As we walked along the road
                with the sunset in our eyes,
                all the world seemed turned to blood
                by the redness of the skies.

Second disciple: And our voices were low,
                and our footsteps were slow,
                we had nowhere to go
                tomorrow.

Cleopas: As we walked along the road
                we were talking of the cross,
                when a stranger heard our sighs
                but knew nothing of our loss.

Second disciple: How the master was dead
                who had offered us bread;
                now we only knew dread
                and sorrow.

Cleopas: As we walked along the road
                he began to speak with power
                of the hidden things of God
                which were destined for this hour.

Second disciple: And he raised our hopes higher,
filled our hearts with strange fire
and rekindled our desire
for living.

Cleopas: When we reached our resting place
we persuaded him to stay,
(though he made as if to go
further on the dusty way).

Second disciple: And the words that he said
as he gave us the bread
made us sure that the dead
was living.

Cleopas: We ran back along the road,
though the stars were in the skies,
ran to tell what we had seen
when the scales fell from our eyes.

Second disciple: And we sang a new song,
as we bounded along,
of the Lord who was strong
and living.

THOMAS

John 20:24-29

If you choose doubting Thomas
    as your patron saint,
    simply because, like you,
    he would only believe
    the things he could touch or see,
    do not then rest
    in agnostic security,
    but remember that, in the end,
    even Thomas was convinced
    by the unexpected evidence of his senses.
And Christ may yet turn
    even *your* doubt into faith,
    by showing you his wounds.

PENTECOST

HOLY SPIRIT

Acts 2:1-4; John 3:8

The Spirit is a lively wind –
   breathtaking
   for those who breathe
   the stale air of mechanical worship;
   but for sails unfurled
   and wings spread wide
   he comes as driving energy,
   uncontrollably bracing.
He only destroys cobwebs
   and dead branches.

The Spirit is a lively power –
   not available
   to bolster up our empires,
   but unpredictably exploding
   in surprising places,
   strengthening weak knees
   and faint hearts,
   and giving secret growth
   to mysterious fruit.
He only destroys
   the rotten enemies
   of our souls.

The Spirit is a lively jester –
  embarrassing,
  with outrageous gesture,
  stiff respectability;
  tumbling over dignity
  in multi-coloured guises,
  impudently prodding
  deadly faces
  into joy and laughter.
He only destroys
  our pomp and vanity.

The Spirit is a lively bee –
  buzzing elusively
  through our solemnities.
He's not pinned down by resolutions,
  but flies in dizzy revolutions
  round our cultivated plots.
Sweet gifts he brings
  of his own making;
  and when he stings,
  his heart is breaking.

PLASTIC GODS

Matthew 3:11; Acts 2:3; Hebrews 12:29

There is a plastic god
    which we have moulded in our image,
    who tolerates our sins,
    flatters our successes,
    gushes over our sadness
    and carpets our path with pleasures,
    demanding only
    superstitious faith
    and pious feelings.
He is a plastic god,
    pre-packed and frozen,
    dehydrated and synthetic;
    available in many holymarkets.

There is a plastic god
    stamped with the mark of the banker,
    bestowing the good things of life
    freely;
    though you pay for them later
    on the day of reckoning.
    (Beware of showing
    too much interest.)

There is also a living God,
    a consuming fire,
    before whom
    plastic melts.

THE PREACHER

Matthew 13:1-9; Mark 4:1-9; Luke 8:4-8; 2 Timothy 4:1-5

A preacher went forth to preach,
  and, as he preached,
  some words fell by the wayside
  into the ears of casual visitors
  to holy places on special occasions;
  and these unprepared strangers
  could not understand the alien language
  of an exclusive religion;
  and they remained unimpressed
  even by the crushing handshakes
  and the hard seats.

And some words fell
  among the sedimentary rocks
  of conventional worship –
  like polished pebbles, echoing and clattering,
  and adding another layer to a dead tradition.

And some words floated like thistledown
  among the prolific weeds
  of humdrum thinking;
  they settled, without taking root,
  among the choking tendrils
  of mediocre expectations.

[Continued

And some words fell onto the good ground
  of minds and hearts
  open, eager and hungry;
  but the words themselves
  were like dry pellets
  that even the birds would spit out –
  pieces of grit, which sometimes sparkle,
  but have no power,
  except to blind searching eyes.

And the preacher returned
  to his lonely chamber
  without even a twofold harvest.

'What use to curse the soil
  if the seed is sterile?'
God told him.
'Come close to me in life and prayer
  and listen for *my* Word;
  look again into the treasury of Scripture
  and I will show you seed
  potent enough to bear fruit
  in all weathers;
  and a lamp bright enough
  to guide the feet of pilgrims
  through the valley of shadows;
  and a sword, sharp enough
  to pierce to the very heart.'

OTHER
OCCASIONS

HARVEST PRAYER

Matthew 6:25-34

Great Lord, our God, we praise you
   for your creative love,
   which made the world around us,
   which made the stars above.
We praise you for all fruitfulness,
   for all that lives and grows;
   for running deer, for flying bird,
   for oak tree and for rose;

   for all the rich variety
   of colour and of form;
   for summer's blazing heat wave
   and for winter's raging storm;
   for every season's beauty,
   for morning and for night,
   for sowing and for reaping,
   for darkness and for light.

We praise you for all sprouting grain,
   for warming sun, refreshing rain,
   for flower and garden, hedge and field,
   for farm's abundant harvest yield;
   for opening buds and hatching eggs,
   for new-born lambs on wobbly legs,
   for freshly wakened butterflies
   and bees that hum beneath blue skies.

Such wealth is ours, O gracious Lord,
  wealth beyond ought we could afford.
Your generous hand supplies our need,
  our bodies and our souls you feed;
  and when adversity's harsh blows
  batter our lives with griefs and woes,
  we learn our greatest need of all –
  for love to hold us lest we fall.
In weakness we would seek your power
  to triumph over each dark hour;
  and praise you still for all your grace
  bestowed upon the human race.

A DREAM OF EDEN

Genesis 2:8-9, 15; 3:23-24; Isaiah 51:3; Revelation 22:1-2

Where trees bear fruit
   and earth yields plant and flower,
   there is a dream of Eden;
   a green memory
   not yet destroyed
   by all the concrete and chemicals
   of Mammon's Utopia.

Where willing backs are bent
   and skilful hands and minds
   share in creative acts with God,
   there is a dream of Eden;
   a vision of a dignity
   not offered by industrial monotony
   and enforced idleness.

Where there is laughter –
   innocent laughter –
   and true enjoyment,
   and honest faith in God,
   there is a dream of Eden;
   a happy echo of God's intention,
   not yet drowned out
   by the vulgar excitements
   of our techno pleasure garden.

For meanwhile, west of Eden,
   ignoring the cherubim
   and the flaming sword,
   we have manufactured our own paradise,
   with plastic fruit
   and fibreglass creatures,
   and electric grottos,
   and polystyrene delights.

Yet God still dreams of Eden,
   and his dreams,
   being greater than our reality
   often surprise us
   by coming true.

ALL SAINTS

John 13:1-7; 14:1-3; Luke 12:37; Matthew 26:26-29

There is a famous hostel,
   where pilgrims reach their goal,
   and standing there to greet them
   with towel and with bowl
   is Christ the mighty traveller,
   the saviour of their race,
   who pioneered their pathway
   and prepared for them a place.

He kneels and pours the water
   on those weary pilgrims' feet,
   to cleanse the dust of ages
   and to cool the angry heat
   of the bruises and the bleeding,
   and to wash away the grime
   that they've picked up on their journey
   through the world of space and time.

So he welcomes them to heaven,
   as he welcomed them on earth,
   with the gift of living water,
   holy sign of their new birth.
And he brings them to the table
   where the heavenly feast is spread,
   and he pours out wine for gladness
   and for love he breaks the bread.
They no longer need the miracle
   of body and of blood,
   for their Host is ever present
   and their souls' sufficient food.

And they do not talk of trial
   or betrayal or arrest;
   there's no mention of denial,
   even by the meanest guest.
For their sins are all forgiven,
   none goes out into the night,
   as they make a full communion
   in the Lord's eternal light.

↓

So he feeds them in the heavens,
   as he fed them on the earth,
   with the holy bread of mercy
   and the wine of holy mirth.

STARS OF HOPE

Matthew 5:16

O God, who said when time did first begin:
   'Let there be light!',
   give us the grace to praise those stars of hope
   who shone by night,
   and in their shining triumphed.

REMEMBRANCE SUNDAY

Luke 19:41-42; 23:27-31

On Remembrance Sunday morning
   as the Legion laid their wreaths,
   I went into the garden
   and I burned the fallen leaves.
I heard the brass band playing
   its slow 'Abide with me'
   and recalled the summer glory
   of the proud and stately tree;
   its branches stark and naked now
   were pointing to the sky,
   but its leaves were drifting earthwards
   to wither and to die.

Where was our help in ages past?
Where is our hope to come?
For all the leaves have fallen,
   and weak is the autumn sun;
   and many were the sons of hope
   nipped from the tree of life
   by the cruel frost of battle
   and the bitter winds of strife.

For war there is no season,
   there is no special hour;
   it takes the tree in winter
   and it takes the fresh spring flower.
And many are the fallen,
   and many are the dead,
   and more will be the autumns
   when the bonfires will be fed.
For even as we honour
   the slaughtered of the past,
   they're burying the victims
   of contemporary blast.

So while the band was playing
   and the Legion laid their wreaths,
   I stood out in the garden
   and I burned the fallen leaves.

THE BIBLE

2 Timothy 3:16-17

(The reader should hold a large black Bible.)

I do not love this book because it is
    black enough to please Puritans,
    holy enough to scare demons,
    thick enough to stop bullets,
    heavy enough to squash flies;
    but because sometimes when I read it
    I am moved
    deeper than tears.

I do not love this book because
    they say it is the very words of God,
    and polish every dot and comma,
    like golden ornaments
    in an idolatrous temple;
    but because sometimes when I read it
    God speaks in a strange tongue
    deeper than words.

I do not love this book because
   the passionate preacher
   beats the truth out of it
   with his blunt fist
   and sharp ideas,
   (for some use the book
   to support their opinions,
   as others might use it
   to support their tables).
But I do love this book
   because sometimes when I read it
   I am disturbed by a truth
   deeper than thought.

And when I read of Jesus,
   then I know,
   that *he* is the Truth
   that moves my soul –
   the living Word of God.

TRANSFIGURATION

Matthew 17:1-20; Mark 9:2-29; Luke 9:28-43

The mountain flames with light
    as Christ, heaven's window,
    opens this dark world
    to divine glory.
He glows with a strange radiance
    normally hidden from earthbound eyes,
    but now revealed
    to dull disciples
    facing the unknown.

And meanwhile,
    down in the valley,
    not lit by other worlds,
    untransfigured suffering
    distorts humanity.
Wretched bearers of pain
    cry out for healing.
Well-meaning helpers
    offer ineffectual suggestions,
    while bystanders move in
    with trivial objections.
Unillumined disciples
    fail
    and turn away,
    embarrassed and ashamed.
Is their faith
    not even the size
    of a mustard seed?

Our earthly light is not enough,
  unless transfigured
  by the light from heaven.
Thank God that Christ's true glory
  was not left to be enshrined
  on some irrelevant mountain top;
  but he came down
  into the valley
  to embrace the human beast
  with arms stretched out
  in sacrificial love,
  that we might share
  his royal beauty,
  and dark earth at last
  be radiant with heaven.

FAITH
AND
PRAYER

AGNOSTIC

Mark 9:24

'The odds on God are even;
   either he is, or he isn't.
It's a fifty-fifty chance;
   hardly worth putting your shirt on,
   let alone staking your body,
   like Christ.
If it's a choice between agony
   and agnosticism,
   give me agnosticism every time.'
So speaks the rationalist in me.

But didn't Christ die for love?
A risky business at the best of times.
And one thing I've learned through life:
   there is no such thing as a safe bet,
   a sure winner;
   except that not to gamble at all
   wins nothing every time.
Argument will get you nowhere.
So try faith.

EYES CLOSED

Matthew 6:5-6

Two people went into a church to pray.
Both bowed their heads,
   and clasped their hands,
   and closed their eyes
   in the usual way.
But one closed his eyes
   to shut out the world
   with its horrors and hate,
   and turned in on himself
   to concentrate
   on his wishes and wants;
   thinking God would be able
   to sort out his problems
   and grant his requests
   with a nod and a wink
   from the holy table.

He would have done better
   to open his eyes
   and to utter no sound,
   but allow God to reach him
   through the wonder and woe
   of the world all around;
   and by making his senses
   a gate open wide, he'd receive what he needed,
   as *God* would decide;
   and his prayer would be answered.

[Continued

111

Now the other one's eyes
   were also shut tight,
   but her reasons were right.
For she knew that the world
   with its bright fascination
   would only disturb
   her soul's deep concentration
   on God and his will.
So in stillness and waiting
   she opened herself
   to the Spirit's dictating.
With eyes closed, she saw,
   and, still loving the world,
   she loved her God more.

THE VITAL THREAD

1 Thessalonians 5:17

The world is hanging by a thread;
   that thread is prayer,
   which links the world
   with God.

LORD, YOU ARE ALL AROUND US

Matthew 18:20

(For up to six readers.)

Lord, you are all around us.
Open our eyes to see –
   in star and mountain, sun and snow;
   in ocean, flower and tree.

Lord, you are all around us.
Help us to understand –
   in speech and music, book and poem;
   in artist's brush and hand.

Lord, you are all around us.
Give us the faith to know –
   in prayer and worship, bread and wine;
   in cross and candle glow.

Lord, you are all around us.
Fill us with love to care –
   for friend and family, stranger and foe;
   our neighbours everywhere.

Lord, you are deep within us.
Move us to live for you –
   give strength and courage, hope and peace,
   in all we are and do.

Lord, you are close beside us.
Lead us in paths of right –
    through joy and sorrow, laughter and tears,
    journeying to the light.

PRAISE

Revelation 4:11

(This could be read by up to six people.)

Lord God, we praise you for your light,
   which gleams and shines in distant stars,
   and streams forth from our neighbour sun,
   bathing in warmth this earth of ours.

Lord God, we praise you for your power,
   which holds the floating worlds in space,
   and lifts the mountains to the sky,
   and keeps the restless sea in place.

Lord God, we praise you for your truth,
   inspiring science, faith and art;
   for every prophet, every saint,
   who stirred the mind or pierced the heart.

Lord God, we praise you for your love,
   which caused this universe to be;
   for true compassion, friendship, care,
   and Christ who died on Calvary.

Lord God, we cannot plumb your depth;
   your height and breadth outstrip our thought.
We bow in penitence and awe,
   for you are all, and we are nought.

Yet, Lord, your light, your power, your truth
   you offer to us for our good;
   and most amazing is your love,
   which Christ has shown us by his blood.

INTERCESSIONS

Ephesians 6:18; Philippians 4:6; Matthew 21:22

Now, as the world rolls on its restless way
  O Lord, we pray;
  for kings and queens and presidents,
  for governors and governments;
  all ministers and cabinets
  all people in authority;
  that when they make decisions
  which affect the lives of millions,
  they may be endowed with wisdom,
  and their hearts moved with compassion,
  as they seek a world where justice
  is applied with proper mercy;
  where the people enjoy freedom,
  yet accept responsibility –
  a world of peace and harmony,
  a world of joy and charity.

Lord, use our human skills of hand and brain
  to feed the hungry mouths and hungry minds;
  to heal the sick and educate the young;
  to cultivate the land and build safe homes;
  to raise the poor from drudgery and want;
  to make, to mine, to transport and to sell,
  with energy, integrity and care.
Help us protect this green oasis world,
  that all may share its beauty and its wealth,
  including generations yet to be.

(Pause for specific prayers for the world.)

Lord, for your Church in every place on earth
   we bring our prayers in fellowship and love.
May those who lead be faithful to their call,
   and use their power to build up and to serve.
May those who preach be faithful to your truth
   and spread the light of Christ in word and life.
Give patience when the Gospel is not heard.
Give strength to those who face a hostile world.
Give hope where failure overrules success,
   and humble awe when thousands crowd your gates.
And in *this* Church, forgive us when we fall
   through lack of faith, or, worse still, lack of love.
Teach us the art of gentle sympathy,
   and offering friendship that is truly meant.
Show us the needs of this community,
   and help us to respond in prayer and deed.
Then may our worship overflow with joy,
   delighting in your presence and your will.

(Pause for specific prayers for the Church.)

Hear our prayers for those who suffer:
   those we know, whose names we whisper
   in our inner heart's devotion;
   and all those whose names we know not,
   but whose pain and grief and troubles
   are already felt in heaven.
Wipe away all tears, our Father.
Lift the downcast, heal the wounded.
Comfort all the broken-hearted
   with the hope that this life's anguish
   can bear fruit in finer spirits
   seeking an eternal Kingdom.

(Pause for specific prayers for individual needs.)

[Continued

119

Lord, receive our prayers and longings;
  all our cares we cast upon you,
  trusting in your love and mercy,
  for the sake of Christ your Son. Amen.

THE GRACE

2 Corinthians 13:14 (RSV, REB and NIV)
2 Corinthians 13:13 (GNB, NRSV and NJB)

May the grace of Christ uphold us.
May the Father's love enfold us.
May the Holy Spirit guide us,
   so that with the Lord beside us,
   we may go our way in peace. Amen.

INDEX

INDEX

The lectionary references which are not marked with asterisks can be found in both the Revised Common Lectionary and the Common Worship Lectionary.

The figures in parentheses ( ) refer to the Proper or Ordinary Time numbering system of the Roman Catholic Church, the Methodist Church in Britain, and the Anglican Church of Canada. Figures in square brackets [ ] refer to Ordinary Time in the Common Worship Lectionary (Church of England).

The capital letters refer to Years A, B and C.

Lectionary references marked with an asterisk * apply to parts of the Common Worship Lectionary used by the Church of England only.

Lectionary references marked with a dagger † are to be found in the parts of the Common Worship Lectionary used by the Church of England and the Methodist Church only.

Lectionary references marked with a double dagger ‡ do not apply to the Church of England.